To my wife Aeyoung and my son Daemian
for their never-ending support and encouragement

© 2011 Alain Greaves ~ easystepsbusinessenglish.com ~ EFL EasySteps Series

How YOU can develop

Effective Business

Email Writing Skills

in English

Alain Greaves

International Business Communications Consultant

CONTENTS

The
EFFECTIVE
BUSINESS
EMAIL
WRITING
FORMULA

IN 7 EASY STEPS

ALAIN GREAVES
EFL EASYSTEPS SERIES

Published by EasySteps Business English ~ 2011

www.easystepsbusinessenglish.com

Copyright Alain Greaves 2006, First Printed Edition 2011

The EasySteps Business English series for ESL / EFL students of business.

Printed in the United States

FOREWORD

Dear Reader,

Would you like to have a simple formula to help you write your email or letter so it is easy for your reader to understand?

Would you like to write your email so that your readers are more likely to take positive action quickly and give you the results you are looking for? If so...

...then this book is for you.

This is not a grammar book or a "teach yourself English" book. Its purpose is to help you think clearly and get the most out of the English you already know. You will find some examples of grammar and vocabulary but only to make it easier for you to understand how to make it more powerful and effective.

*When you have a message to deliver, you nearly always want your reader to **do** something, to take some action, even if that action is to wait and **do nothing**.*

I developed this simple formula for myself when I was running my media company to make sure all my messages had the maximum power to get the results I wanted, quickly and easily.

It has saved me an enormous amount of time and helped me remember vital information on many occasions. In fact, it has enabled me to get where I wanted to go and achieve the success in my businesses by virtually **guaranteeing results**.

Even if you are not running your own business, climbing the corporate ladder can be uncertain unless you are someone who knows how to **get the job done**.

Do you know what companies are looking for when choosing to promote people, or when they are taking on new staff for managerial or executive positions?

In a survey in the USA in 2006, senior executives reported that a person's chance of getting the job or promotion depended on only two main factors.

The first was the ability to do the work well (15% importance) and the second was the ability to communicate effectively and powerfully (85% importance).

This is a clear indication that your ability to communicate effectively and powerfully to **get the job done** is much more important than any of your other skills.

Did you also know that you can learn to write very much better just by using the **English you already know…**

…more effectively?

The purpose of this book is to show you that it is not essential to be **PERFECT** at English to communicate well. This book will lead you step by step through a process, which will make it **EASY** for you to develop your writing skills no matter what your current level of English. This will not only make you more effective **immediately** but also help you with your study of English.

It should prove useful to you, whether you are a native or non-native speaker of English. It is a formula for making sure that, if you follow the step-by-step process every time you write, you will think about all the important factors during the preparation of your email.

It applies to most forms of your written communication:

Emails...

        Letters...

                Faxes...

                        Memos...

You will have to work at it but, with practice, you will definitely learn to write more quickly, more effectively, and be able to get the job done.

Try it and see the results for yourself.

Alain Greaves

GETTING THE JOB DONE

My father was the managing director of a small manufacturing firm that made all kinds of building products out of wrought iron, such as fire escapes, gates, railings, and fences.

As a small boy I would go with him to his office on Saturday mornings and watch him working. His routine was to answer all the remaining letters he had received that he had not been able to reply to during the week, and he gave me my first lessons in business writing.

I followed his style of writing when I started my own business but quickly realised that, although it had worked well for him, it was old fashioned and was not very effective for the modern business age.

I looked around for quicker and more efficient ways to communicate in writing and found very few people locally who could advise me. Eventually I decided to look at people who were already very successful in the business world to see if I could model what they were doing.

Once I realised that information about business communication was available in books and on audiotape from people like Brian Tracy, Jim Rohn and Jay Abraham, I began listening to everything I could get my hands on. I was hungry for knowledge and was convinced I could grow my business if I could improve my communication skills. I had this insatiable curiosity to discover the secrets of business success.

I'm sure you must have had similar feelings at one time or another when you would have given anything to know how something was done.

The excitement of discovery is extremely inspiring, such as the moment I realised that I could be good at history. My usual history teacher made every lesson excruciatingly boring. He would write endlessly on the chalkboard and we had to copy everything he had written. As a result my handwriting became very bad because I rushed to get all the words into my notebook and I was always bottom of the class at history.

Then for some reason my usual teacher took some time off and we had a new teacher take over. She told us stories and formed us into groups of 'Romans' and 'Anglo-Saxons'. We played games, learning how castles were built and defended in battles, and I became incredibly excited by it all.

Suddenly history had come alive and become great fun, not like learning at all. I feel sure you have experienced that feeling of having fun when ideas and understanding become so clear that you don't realise you are actually studying.

I remember wondering what my exam results would be like as we waited for the teacher to put the scores on the classroom wall, but most of all I knew that history could be really exciting, challenging and terrific fun. Just like how I felt about distance running.

I had been a distance runner for several years and it was time for the annual cross-country race at my school. I had always been the best runner in my grade and I felt that as long as I kept up my strength and determination I would win again this year.

The gun went off and about 150 boys rocketed across the playing fields to the gate that would funnel us out into the countryside in a battle of strength and stamina. I was leading the charge as usual, keeping a sharp eye on my closest rival, Richard, by my right shoulder, who had sworn to beat me this year. We exchanged the lead several times as we fought neck-and-neck around the punishing course. Eventually, we shot out of the narrow alley onto the bottom of the final steep hill leading to the downhill stretch that would bring us back to the school gates and the comfort of the finishing tape.

It was at this point that all the fun seemed to disappear when Richard kicked forward leaving me as if I was standing still. He seemed to have been given a rocket boost and I found myself struggling just to keep going. Suddenly my legs felt like jelly and my lungs were bursting. I could see Richard way in front reaching the top of the hill and I knew he was too far ahead for me to challenge his lead. I kept at it, but after rounding the corner at the top, I could see him, now so far in front, that I couldn't imagine how I could possibly catch him.

My desire to win was almost dead. My instinct told me I had lost at this event for the first time but in my head a little voice kept saying, "If you really challenge yourself and if you want it badly enough you might still have a chance."

We really have to challenge ourselves if we wish to achieve the success we deserve. Communicating well is always a challenge too, even for native speakers.

Everyone who is not a native speaker seems to be studying English these days. It may be because it is essential for good communications in the International Business marketplace, but few people realise that a high standard of English skill is no guarantee of winning the contract or being successful in business.

Even native English speakers do not always communicate effectively!

When marketing, selling, negotiating, presenting, or simply talking to a colleague it is not how perfectly you say or write something, but how the listener or reader understands the message.

Is the **understanding** of the listener or reader **always** equal to the **intention** of the speaker or writer?

The answer is a resounding NO!!

When taking part in a conversation it is quite easy for the speaker to see and feel whether the listener has understood, because of immediate feedback.

However, when a reader is trying to understand a written message there are no gestures, facial expressions, movement, voice tones or pauses to help.

The reader has only the words and the structure to work with and the writer must wait for the reader's reply to find out if the writer's **intention** has been fully **understood** by the reader.

Do YOU get the job done?

To get the job done, whether you are native or non-native speakers of English, you must generate good working relationships with your business colleagues and associates.

This is commonly called rapport.

This book will help you to understand more fully the 'ART' of communication and how it depends on your **attitude** more than your English skill. It will help you to build rapport and get results.

© 2011 Alain Greaves ~ easystepsbusinessenglish.com ~ EFL EasySteps Series

Continue, of course, to develop your English and to achieve an ever-increasing command of the language, but by adopting a modern, systematic and positive business approach, you can learn to use the level of English you already have...

...more powerfully...

...more effectively...

...to get the job done...

...and achieve greater success in your chosen field.

Why Is Effective Business Email Writing Important?

The written word is a vital means of communication in today's business environment.

We communicate by email internally and internationally as well as by letter and memo to convey our messages to others.

By working through this 7 Step course you will be able to assess the effectiveness of your own business email writing, and to learn to communicate with others more appropriately and successfully. (Note that reports and technical papers are written differently and this formula was designed to be used when you are communicating directly with specific people.)

It will help you to develop understanding and skills to achieve greater impact and quality in all your written communications.

My goal is to 'make it easy' for you to use and develop your writing skills using your **current level of English**.

By following the ideas in this book you will be able to:

- Use the most effective structures and formats for both formal, and informal emails, which means your writing will always be appropriate for the situation.
- Present information in a way that is more attractive and easier to understand for your readers, which means they will welcome your emails and feel good about reading them.
- Identify and meet the needs of your reader, which is the key to persuading your reader to give you what you want.
- Understand how your choice of language and style can help you achieve greater success when you need to inform, influence or persuade your reader.
- You will build a reputation as both an excellent communicator and someone who **gets the job done.**

What Is Communication?

To communicate in the best possible way, we must first define communication, so here is a simple and concise definition.

Good communication is the…

…effective exchange of information, ideas and emotion.

Now let's look at what we mean by each word in the definition.

Effective

If your communication is not effective then you may need to send and receive many additional emails so you and your reader can fully understand each other and act effectively in the situation.

© 2011 Alain Greaves ~ easystepsbusinessenglish.com ~ EFL EasySteps Series

Exchange

Your communication must also be two-way, otherwise it will simply be one side taking instructions from the other.

To be effective the people involved will create better results by sharing and listening to each other before making decisions and taking action.

When people give no feedback or delay it, the other person has no idea what is happening, which may cause additional and unnecessary problems.

Information

Data, specifications, etc., are the usual first thought when thinking about your communication. The person who initiates the communication is usually focused only on their own message and very often does not consider how it may affect the receiver.

Ideas

The way we think and the ideas we have are basic ingredients in successful business. You must enable the other person to clearly understand your ideas in the shortest possible time.

If the person does not understand the benefits of your ideas then your excellent suggestion may be lost, possibly forever.

Emotion

The final ingredient in any communication is our emotional content. We often transmit how we are currently feeling to the receiver through the style of language we use and may cause our reader confusion without realising it ourselves.

In addition, it is often very difficult to think clearly and communicate well when our emotions are getting in the way.

Your emotional condition can be a barrier
to effective communications, because it
may change the way you create your email.

TIP:

This will help you make your email more **Effective** and make it easier to **Exchange** your **Information** and **Ideas.**

It will also help you minimise the effect of how you are feeling (**Emotion**) on your writing style, when you are trying to compose a written communication in English.

K I S S

KEEP IT SHORT & SIMPLE

This has been the advice to speakers and writers for centuries.

Time is our most valuable asset and we should use it as if it were **gold**.

People do not want to waste their time reading and working through unnecessary material.

Most people prefer to know just the key points and as long as they can do the job with the information they have been given, they are usually happy.

THE EASYSTEPS
7-STEP FORMULA

STEP 1:
CLARIFY YOUR PURPOSE

Make sure you know exactly
why you are writing

'Of course I know why I am writing,' you are probably thinking to yourself.

It might seem like an unnecessary question, but if we examine the usual trend in writing we find that many people forget the most crucial part of their message.

They often give large amounts of unnecessary or repetitive detail, which confuses or bores the reader.

Surveys done in the UK and USA have shown that as much as 73% of communications are either *unnecessary* or *ineffective*.

This is a waste of your reader's time and yours.

Imagine you get an email from a colleague asking you for information about a meeting that took place last month. He has not told you which meeting he is thinking of or what it was about.

He assumes you know automatically, which meeting he is referring to. However, you realise from the information he has told you he needs, it could be one of three different meetings. You now have to write back to find out which meeting he means.

The first step in reducing the number of unnecessary emails from going back and forth, (what I call 'Ping Pong'), is for each writer to spend a little more time in considering the purpose of your email and what outcome is wanted.

If you consider what your reader already knows about the subject and check previous emails between you both, you can save hours of delay and prevent 'Ping Pong.'

The following questions will help you to assess your purpose in writing your email.

✓ **What is *my* main reason for writing this email?**

✓ **What outcome do *I expect* from this email?**

✓ **What outcome will *my reader expect* from this email?**

✓ **What does my reader *already* know about this situation?**

✓ **What will my reader *need* to be able to do what I am asking?**

✓ **How will my reader *feel* about this email?**

✓ **Will *my reader's understanding* be the same as *my intention*?**

The answers to these questions will help you to focus more clearly on the purpose of your email and increase its power to get your job done.

However, I hear some of you already complaining that you don't have enough time to write your email, never mind go through what seems to be a long checklist and this step-by-step approach.

Your boss is screaming at you to get the email out and you can't see a way to do it quickly if you use this method.

I fully understand your problem and it will take some discipline from you to raise the standard of your writing, but consider the following points:

✓ **If you continue doing it the same old way you will probably not improve much and the results will be the same as they have always been.**

✓ **On the other hand, if you make some effort to master these simple techniques then…**

…you will soon begin writing more quickly…

…the quality of your writing will improve…

…you will get faster replies and better outcomes from your readers and…

…your reputation in your job will improve.

Sometimes you must take a small amount of pain at first to make things better for yourself in the future.

Improvement in anything will require you to put in some extra effort and becoming good at writing is no exception.

I believe you will make it easier for yourself by using this formula rather than spending many long hours just studying English Grammar with no guarantee of improving your communication skills.

Grammar is important and should not be neglected, but you may be surprised to learn that you can **do a lot more** with what you **already know** without the need to study more grammar, if you **learn to use what English you already know more effectively.**

STEP 2:
KNOW YOUR READER

Why you must get to know your reader

Of course you know who your reader is. True, you should know your reader's name and may have written to them many times in the past, but the point here is to consider what difference it might make if your reader is either older or younger than you, or in a higher or lower position in the company.

✓ **Is your reader familiar with your area of skill in your job?**

✓ **Will your reader understand the special terms you use?**

✓ **What formality is appropriate?**

You would be unlikely to write the same email to the CEO of another company as you would to a sales person in your own company, even though the topic might be the same.

The approach, style, formality, and focus would be different.

✓ **If you are writing about the launch of a new product by your company and your reader is a sales person they are likely to be interested in Features, Benefits, Price, Service, Warranties, etc.**

✓ **If your reader is from the finance department, the most important points might be Costs and Profits, even though the topic is the same.**

Usually a quick mental check will cover this point and you can quickly move on to the next step.

However, when writing to someone for the first time, this step will require you to do some homework.

Part of being successful in your business communications is for you to build a good working relationship with the other person.

Business is not really about companies but about the **people** who make the business happen. Making that all-important 'good first impression' has to be your first goal.

Creating a good working relationship with your reader can make a huge difference in you getting the job done and winning their support in times of crisis.

This is where the most important part of communications skill, 'TONE', comes in. It is the least understood of all areas of writing and often the most difficult to grasp.

However, if you can write with good tone you have the key to a successful outcome.

Once you 'get it' you will improve your chances of getting a good result every time you write.

Set the right tone

You should build successful relationships and create excellent rapport that will be of tremendous help to you in getting the job done!

As already stated, your tone is extremely important because you are working with another person and business will generally go very much better when those involved get on well together.

It is not necessary for you to become personal friends with your reader but a close working relationship will speed up mutual understanding and make your business life more pleasant.

Choose the right words to create a positive feeling

At school, most people learn long lists of words to increase their English vocabulary. Whilst this can be beneficial, trying to remember how to use those words correctly may not be so easy.

Your aim should be to use the simplest and most effective words to achieve the right tone for the occasion.

Avoid 'Old fashioned' or 'Text book' wording

Wording style is changing all the time and what was normal a few years ago may now be 'old fashioned' and awkward.

Wording that was used 50 or 100 years ago is now out-dated and much too long for modern fast business use.

Examples:

Poor: I trust that we will be able to meet again soon.

Better: *I look forward to seeing you soon.*

Poor: Attached you will find the report you requested.

Better: *The report you requested is attached*

Poor: I trust that you have duly received the sales figures.

Better: *I sent you the sales figures yesterday.*

Poor: We have duly received the monthly report.

Better: *Thank you for the monthly report*

Poor: When the ietm arrives, kindly advise us.

Better: *Please tell us/Please let us know when the item arrives*

Poor: Please be advised that the sales meeting is on Friday.

Better: *The sales meeting is on Friday.*

However, this book will show you how to improve your writing even more.

STEP 3:
WRITE YOUR OPENING

Create Rapport

The opening paragraph of your email is crucial in making sure your reader will go on to read the whole document and then do what you want them to do.

The purpose of the opening is to introduce the main theme in a way that will interest and stimulate your reader.

The common fault is making the opening too long and filling it with uninteresting and unnecessary detail.

Open dynamically
to grab the attention of your reader.

Your first objective is to get your reader to read your email and take action to do whatever you have requested.

To get your reader to do this you have to GRAB their attention immediately. Make it interesting and give them some 'Reader Benefit' (see later).

Focus on them (the YOU attitude: see later) so they will continue reading through to the closing paragraph.

Maintain the
'Seven Cs' standards

The following key points will help you to assess your own writing and can be used as a checklist when writing anything.

If your writing meets all the 'Seven Cs' standards then it is most likely to be acceptable to your reader.

1. Clear

Clarity is the cornerstone of success. If your email is not clear then the chances of you getting the result you want may be very small.

State exactly what you mean without any extra unnecessary information. Be direct and simple.

Ask yourself the question: "Will my reader be CLEAR about my intentions?"

Clarity will also be improved if your email follows the next four points, **correct, complete, concrete and concise**.

Write exactly what you mean and make it easy to understand.

Poor: Let's have lunch sometime.

Better: *Let's have lunch tomorrow at 12:30 in Chez Nous next to your office.*

2. Correct

Don't guess anything. Make sure all information is correct and confirmed.

Incorrect information can cause a lot of confusion and waste time.

Poor: I think the meeting starts around 2:00.

Better: **I just checked and the meeting is scheduled to start at 2:30pm.**

3. Complete

Your email must be sufficiently complete for the receiver to be able to act and get the job done.

If a vital piece of information is missing then your reader will have a problem and maybe so will you.

Poor: Send me the information on the London project.

Better: **Please send me the financial report and the planning schedule on the London project.**

4. Concrete

Your email should be specific, solid and easy to understand.

Don't be philosophical as the receiver may not fully understand and do the wrong thing.

Poor: The client wants to know more about what is happening with this project.

Better: **The client would like to know if we will meet the agreed schedule.**

5. Concise

Concise is more than just short. It is the **'maximum amount of information in the minimum number of words.'**

It will help the receiver to understand your email more easily as there will be less chance for misunderstanding.

Poor: I know there have been lots of people wondering just what might be happening after the project is finished but I'm sure they will all get to know what has happened, when they read the report they will be sent once the project has been completed.

Better: **All interested parties will be sent an up-to-date report when the project is complete.**

6. Courteous

Being courteous is not exactly the same as being polite.

Courteous means 'from the heart' and should reflect a positive and polite attitude to your receiver. It should make them feel that you care about them and their situation.

Poor: The report must be completed by Friday noon.

Better: **Please make sure the report is completed by Friday noon.**

7. Conversational

Conversational is not the same as having a conversation. When talking, we use extra phrases, words and pauses for 'thinking time' because we construct our sentences as we go along.

Thinking time expressions are used to give the speaker time to consider what their next key point might be and usually don't add any real value to the conversation.

On the other hand, *conversational* means that the communication feels like a relaxed conversation but without all the unnecessary extra words and phrases.

When writing you do not need to include the 'thinking time' expressions, as they have no real meaning for your reader.

This type of expression is often unnecessary:
"As you already know…"
"…and let me be clear about this…"

Key points for creating great opening paragraphs:

Work with the following list to write a direct attention grabbing paragraph and you will be assured of a more positive reaction from your reader.

✓ **Always begin with Good News.**

Get your reader into a relaxed and comfortable mood by referring to something positive that leads into the reason for your email.

✓ **If there is any Bad News then you should introduce it gently second.**

The opening of any email is crucial in making sure your reader will go on to read the whole document and then do what you want them to do. Introduce any bad news gently so as not to shock your reader, then...

✓ **Follow up with a Solution or something positive.**

Always leave your reader with as positive a feeling as possible. It is difficult for people to be effective when they are upset.   If you need the help of your reader, save the discussion about who is to blame until the job is done.

✓ **Construct meaningful sentences without repetition.**

When we initially write, the result will usually have a lot of repetition. Either the same word is used many times or the same idea is written in several different ways, sometimes even in the same sentence. To be meaningful to your reader, editing your work to remove repetition will greatly shorten your email and make it clearer and easier to understand.

© 2011 Alain Greaves ~ easystepsbusinessenglish.com ~ EFL EasySteps Series

Building a good relationship requires you to approach your reader with a positive TONE.

To achieve this you must focus on:

- ✓ **The 'YOU Attitude'**

- ✓ **'Reader Benefit'**

- ✓ **Being Positive**

- ✓ **MINIMUM Detail**

Let's look at each one in turn.

The 'YOU attitude'

In most English speaking countries people are proud of their name. They expect you to know it and be able to spell and pronounce it correctly.

However, you can't use their name in every sentence or paragraph when writing, as it would seem ridiculous.

In advertising, it has been noted that the two most used words in English are 'YOU' and 'YOUR' and when you use either of these the connection to your reader is dramatically increased as it is the nearest you can get to using their name.

'You' and 'your' are almost as good as using the person's name.

Poor Example:

I got your email about the problem.

The focus here is on 'I'.

This is easy to improve and refocus from your reader's point of view.

Improvement:

*Thank **you** for **your** email about **your** problem.*

Your reader may not realise it, but you have just made them feel more important.

This is a huge improvement with only a small change to the wording.

Exercises:

Try to change the following sentences and focus on the reader's point of view instead of the writer's.

(See appendix for suggested answers)

We wish to announce our new product range.

_____

_____

_____

We will be happy to email the contract details.

_____

_____

_____

We must have your proposal immediately.

_____

_____

_____

However, sometimes you can focus strongly on your reader **without** using the words 'you' or 'your'.

Poor Example:

I think you should accept our proposal.

Again the focus here is on 'I'.

Improvement:

Please consider our proposal.

Although the word 'you' has not been used, the word 'please' has a strong connection with the person and gives the feeling of the 'You attitude'.

Exercises:

Try to change the following sentences and focus on the reader's point of view instead of the writer's.

(See appendix for suggested answers)

I want you to come to our office next week.

_____

_____

_____

I recommend you to call Mr. Jones at ABC.

_____

_____

_____

We expect you to deliver on time.

_____

_____

_____

We can meet you in Munich at the exhibition.

_____

_____

_____

'You Attitude' Vs 'You Approach'

However:

Simply using the word you is not a guarantee of success. Sometimes using the **You Approach** does not produce the **You Attitude.**

Poor Example:

You didn't send us the information you promised us last week. (You approach)

The **approach** here is using the word **you** but the focus is on how the reader has **failed**.

It could upset the reader and damage the relationship.

Even if the statement is true, a more pleasant approach could be used to let the reader know there is a problem without blaming them.

Improvement:

Please send us the information you promised us last week, so that we can (do this for you)... *(You attitude, plus indicating a benefit for the reader)*

This improves the chances of a good response from the reader because it is simply restating the request. This focuses the reader on the next action step and not on their mistake or problem.

Exercises:

Try to change the following sentences and focus on the 'YOU attitude' not the 'YOU approach' without offending the reader.

You misunderstood the specifications.

_____

_____

_____

You failed to include the sample.

_____

_____

_____

You must meet our deadline.

_____

_____

_____

You can't attend the meeting on Friday.

_____

_____

_____

You didn't complete the order.

_____

_____

_____

You told us the attachment was corrupted.

_____

_____

_____

You should send us the data we want.

_____

_____

_____

You should work with us on the ABC problem.

_____

_____

_____

Your information is wrong.

_____

_____

_____

You confused me with your report.

_____

_____

_____

You made a mistake on the contract.

_____

_____

_____

You are requested to complete the attached form.

_____

_____

_____

You forgot to send the attachment.

_____

_____

_____

Reader Benefit

What exactly is 'Reader Benefit?'

A very experienced businessperson once said; *"If you give people what they want, they will give you what you want."*

Therefore, 'Reader Benefit' is the answer to the question; **"Can I give my reader something they want, so that they will give me what I want?"**

Many people may think that 'Reader Benefit' must be something like:

Lower prices, faster delivery, reliability, service, quality, stability, convenience, environmental protection, comfort, enjoyment, health, savings, satisfaction, extended warranty, etc.

It is true that these could all be 'Reader Benefits,' but very often…

✓ **Thank you for the information you sent.**

✓ **I appreciate your situation.**

✓ **I am looking carefully at your proposal.**

✓ **We will make a quick decision.**

…are just what the reader wants to know and can be very powerful 'Reader Benefits.'

© 2011 Alain Greaves ~ easystepsbusinessenglish.com ~ EFL EasySteps Series

Exercises:

Try rewriting the following sentences to improve the 'YOU' attitude and add your own 'Reader Benefit' to encourage your reader to give you what you want.

You are requested to activate the contract by signing the enclosed copy and returning it to us promptly.

_____

_____

_____

The specifications are inadequate and we expect you to give us more detail.

_____

_____

_____

You made a mistake in your calculations and you have to work with us to put them right.

_____

_____

_____

We can't make a decision unless you give us all the information we need.

_____

_____

_____

We won't be able to deliver on time unless you send us the Letter of Credit quickly.

_____

_____

_____

Be Positive

The 'YOU' attitude and 'Reader Benefit' are the two most important ways of preparing your reader to give you what you want. If you add a positive way of writing to that, instead of a negative method, the power and effectiveness of your email will almost certainly motivate your reader to give you what you want.

Example:

It isn't possible to meet the deadline unless the problem of transportation is solved.

Improvement:

Your deadline can be met as long as a transport solution can be found.

This is now focusing on what can be done and what is needed to allow it to happen.

Exercises:

Try rewriting the following sentences to transform them into more positive statements.

Also improve the 'YOU' attitude and 'Reader Benefit' where appropriate.

We cannot deliver the order until July 21.

_____

_____

_____

Your specifications are incomplete so we are unable to make a decision.

_____

_____

_____

We are sorry to say, but we cannot reduce the price more than 7%.

_____

_____

_____

You didn't give us all the details so we can't quote on the project.

_____

_____

_____

Because your terms were not in writing, we cannot accept responsibility for the breakages.

_____

_____

_____

We cannot allow you to return this equipment because it has been damaged.

_____

_____

_____

Your quotation was delayed so we cannot submit it for consideration.

_____

_____

_____

Unless you agree to our terms you will not be able to import these goods.

_____

_____

_____

Keep detail to a minimum

The final key to a successful and attention-grabbing opening is that you keep it SHORT.

Remember the K I S S tip

Focus on the issues and only add the details later, in either the detail paragraphs or the closing.

You must create impact and to do that effectively your opening paragraph should contain 'Reader Benefit', focus on the 'YOU' attitude, give a positive focus, (even when bringing Bad News) and keep detail to a minimum.

STEP 4:
WRITE YOUR CLOSING

Call for action

Most people would probably write the detail next, but in my formula the closing paragraph of your email is often best written before the detail paragraphs.

This is because it is the second most important part and should state the next step for both you and your reader.

In addition, in email writing we usually already know what action we want our reader to take or what the next step is likely to be.

You should therefore explain in the closing what action comes next, when it should be done and how.

It should also contain reader benefit, as well as something positive and it is your last chance to get your reader to act or react to your requests.

Once you have written the closing it will help you to keep the detail short and focused only on the essential information detail.

Close powerfully
to motivate your reader to act.

Your final paragraph, called the closing, is your last opportunity to motivate your reader. It should be written using the 'YOU attitude' and should include Reader Benefit.

Focus on the following questions:

WHAT?   What happens next?

Your reader should have a good idea what you want by now, but the closing paragraph is where you can give the specific details.

State clearly and simply what you want.

Examples:

…please sign and return the contract….

…let me know what you think of….

WHEN?   *When should it happen?*

Your reader wants you to make it easy to act and will be grateful if you can give specific dates and times. You must be courteous and include reasons (see Why? following) to motivate your reader to act quickly and positively

Examples:

...by Friday, January 25....

...by close of business Monday June 21....

WHERE?   *Where should it happen?*

If you miss out important information your reader may not take the action you need. Adding details about where things should be sent, even if your reader already knows, confirms and strengthens your case for a positive result.

Examples:

…send your sample to the R&D department….

…let's meet at your office….

HOW?   How should it happen?

By giving your reader exact instructions on how you would prefer the action to take place you are helping your reader to act by making it easier for them.

It also increases your chances of getting the result you want via your own preferred method.

Examples:

…by express delivery service….

…by phoning me on 02 3456 7890….

WHO?   *Who is involved?*

If there are other people involved you may need to give extra details to your reader about them to make sure everyone is kept informed. Always remember to tell your reader if you are the one who will take the action.

Examples:

...Mr. Bryant will call you to confirm the delivery has been received....

...I will send you the details....

WHY?   *Why should your reader do it?*

Without any doubt this is the most important question to answer. This is the reason or motivation for your reader to act. By being very clear and courteous here you can get your reader to do what you want quickly, because it will be **in your reader's interest** to do so.

Examples:

...so that you can....

...to make sure you get a quick decision....

Finally

This is your opportunity to express
something positive about the future.

Examples:

*We look forward to meeting you at the
convention next month.*

*We feel sure this ABC project will be a great
success and hope to cooperate with you for
many future contracts.*

STEP 5:
DECIDE YOUR DETAIL

Read your email through carefully

Ask yourself the following question.

Is there enough information in my opening and closing paragraphs for my reader to do what needs to be done?

- ✓ If the answer is NO then you must write the detail paragraphs.

- ✓ If the answer is YES then you can move straight to STEP 6.

Write Your Detail in
the Detail Paragraphs

Write the Detail with only essential information in the minimum number of words.

If the information in the opening and closing paragraphs is **not** enough for your reader to do what you want done, then you must add the necessary information between the opening and closing.

This is called the detail and each topic should be in a separate paragraph.

Make sure you give only essential information and focus on making it easy for your reader to understand.

Each main topic should be in a separate paragraph. Each paragraph should be made up of one or more sentences, with each sentence within the paragraph focusing on one idea related to the main topic of that paragraph.

Your paragraphs should be short and probably no more than five sentences.

If the paragraph is longer than this it may be possible to separate it into two or more paragraphs of different topics.

How to create effective sentences:

To make your email more powerful and effective you should use the basic form of sentence construction.

✓ **Always begin with your Subject (Who or what is your main focus),**

✓ **Then your Verb (The action taking place) and**

✓ **Next your Object (Who or what is receiving the action).**

✓ Finally you can consider how to modify or qualify each part of the sentence to give the detail needed.

Example:

In this sentence a clause has been placed before the subject:

Regarding the ABC project, we will start it as soon as we have received the reply with the signed contract and the amended specifications.

Improvement:

To make this sentence more effective the subject should be first:

We will start the ABC project as soon as your signed contract and the amended specifications arrive.

The sentence is not only more effective but shorter and can more easily be focused using the 'You' attitude.

Organise topics into paragraphs to make it easy to read.

If you group your related ideas into properly formed paragraphs will make your overall message more logical and therefore easier for your reader to understand.

It will also help your reader to find each topic when rereading your email later.

How to create effective paragraphs:

Paragraphs help you to organise your thoughts into a logical pattern.

Each paragraph should focus on a single topic to make it easier for your reader to identify the key points of your email.

Each sentence in the paragraph should relate to the key topic of that paragraph.

Paragraphs must follow a logical pattern if you want to make it easy for your reader to understand the situation and respond in a quick and positive manner.

In the following example, you can see how the paragraph is too long and should be broken into smaller ones. In the improved version, each sentence is clearly related to the paragraph topic and adds to your reader's overall understanding.

Example:

Enclosed are all the samples you asked us to provide for your R & D department to test. They include the auxiliary components and conform to the technical specifications that you asked for at our meeting in Geneva last month. Thank you again for taking your time to appraise our products for your upcoming project. The additional specifications and pricing structure will be available next week. Please contact me on 02 3456 7890 should you have any questions or wish to arrange our meeting after your R&D have done their assessment.

Improvement:

Enclosed are all the samples you asked us to provide for your R & D department to test. They include the auxiliary components and conform to the technical specifications that you asked for at our meeting in Geneva last month.

Thank you again for taking your time to appraise our products for your upcoming project. The additional specifications and pricing structure will be available next week.

Please contact me on 02 3456 7890 should you have any questions or to wish arrange our meeting after your R&D have done their assessment.

Once you have completed your writing steps:

Read your email OUT LOUD.

When you read something **OUT LOUD** it is easier to pick up on any mistakes, because your brain is active in three areas instead of one.

You read with your eyes (using brain area 1) and your brain sends the signal to your voice (using brain area 2). Then your ears (using brain area 3) pick up the sound of your voice. Each area uses a different part of your brain so you have three times the opportunity of finding a mistake.

You are looking for logical flow and your email must make sense.

You can do this by making sure your email follows the "Seven Cs" standards:

1. **Clear**
2. **Correct**
3. **Complete**
4. **Concrete**
5. **Concise**
6. **Courteous**
7. **Conversational**

Based on reading your email out loud you will be ready for **Step Six.**

STEP 6:
EDIT YOUR EMAIL

Improve quality and effectiveness

Some people enjoy finding fault with the writing they receive. Your email may be ignored if the **way** you have presented it becomes more interesting and maybe amusing to your reader than the information contained in it.

By carefully editing your email you can improve its quality and effectiveness.

Therefore you should check the following areas:

Words and phrases

Amend or replace your words and phrases and adjust the order in which your information is presented, to follow the Seven Cs standards explained earlier.

Avoid using the same phrases or words too many times by finding alternative ways to say something if it needs repeating.

Paragraphing

Keep each topic in a separate paragraph and make each paragraph follow on logically from the previous one.

Check your Grammar

Use your dictionary and grammar references to ensure your verbs are in the appropriate tenses and relate correctly to each other.

Check your prepositions and articles carefully.

Spelling

Use your dictionary as well as your computer's spellcheck system to avoid making spelling errors.

However do not rely on the computer to find all the errors. The computer can only indicate words or phrases that fail to obey certain rules set up in the application you are using. If the rules are very simple then the computer may not pick up even some basic errors. In the end you are responsible for editing.

Capitals

Make sure that the first word of each sentence begins with a capital. Look at any abbreviations you may have used and check people's names.

Spacing

Look at your email to make sure each part is in a separate paragraph.

STEP 7:
CHECK AGAIN
BEFORE YOU SEND

Read Out Loud

Finally read your email again OUT LOUD as your last check

If your email is really important ask a colleague to read it through also, as this may reveal misunderstandings or misinterpretations that you just don't notice yourself.

Your chances of getting the result you want

will have been dramatically increased

if you follow these 7 steps.

THE 7 EASYSTEPS SUMMARY

STEP 1: Clarify Your Purpose

Make sure you know exactly why you are writing

STEP 2: Know Your Reader

Why you must get to know your reader

STEP 3: Write Your Opening

Create Rapport

The 'YOU attitude'

Reader Benefit

Be Positive

Keep detail to a minimum

STEP 4: Write Your Closing

Call for action

STEP 5: Decide Your Detail

Read your email through carefully

Write your detail in the Detail Paragraphs

STEP 6: Edit Your Email

Improve quality and effectiveness

STEP 7: Check Again Before You Send

Read out loud

© 2011 Alain Greaves ~ easystepsbusinessenglish.com ~ EFL EasySteps Series

WRAPPING IT ALL UP

Now that you have the 7-Step Formula you are ready to make every piece of your writing an excellent communication that should inspire your reader to take positive and immediate action and give you what you want to get your job done.

You can always improve if you want it badly enough. Which brings me back to how I was feeling as I watched Richard racing down the hill toward the finishing line. I really wanted to win this race and even though I felt exhausted and all seemed lost I decided to give it my best shot.

I kicked hard and chased after him. I guess he was going flat out because at first I didn't seem to get any nearer. Then as the entrance to the school playing fields came into view I knew this was my last chance. I kicked really hard again and this time as he turned into the last 50-metre stretch he appeared to be getting a little closer. I heard a little voice in my head, which said, "you can do it if you really want it badly enough."

So, I kicked for the third and last time and realised I was only 10 metres behind.

Richard and I crossed the line together but I leaned forward to break the tape with my chest and receive the winner's rosette. I must have really wanted it badly.

Discovering our hidden talents can be one of the most exciting and inspiring processes. Realising that History was not a boring subject but full of interesting and exciting stories of how things were done and how people lived had inspired me to get involved and learn more. Suddenly History lessons had become great fun, not like learning at all.

We had all been inspired by our new teacher and when our exam results were posted on the classroom wall we were all eager to see our score.

It was truly remarkable. The whole class had improved dramatically but what astounded me most was what I had achieved. I was equal top scorer with another student who was always top of the class in History. Having fun while learning had truly paid off.

When I realised that I would have to improve my communication skills to make my business successful I decided to enjoy the process and developed a truly ferocious curiosity. I read and studied everything I could get my hands on to improve my skills.

I created my own system, taking what I could from all the communications experts I could find, and organised it into the simple 7-Step Formula you have just read.

If you want to win badly enough; if you can enjoy the process and make it fun; if you are so curious that you are prepared to seek out information from many different places, then you will definitely improve your communication skills and achieve the success you are looking for.

I truly wish you all the very best,

Alain Greaves

APPENDIX

Format

What is formatting?

Formatting covers **four** main areas of your email:

Order

What comes first, what comes second, etc?
Address, Name, Date, etc.

Spacing

How many spaces between the parts?

Alignment

Justified left, right or both sides, centred or a mixture?

Form

How should the date be shown?

How should your email end?

Why is formatting essential?

Firstly it makes your email look professional.

Also, good formatting makes your email easier to read.

Finally it makes it easier for your reader to find the important parts of your email when re-reading it.

How a business email is formatted

Date:

Unnecessary as each email is automatically dated

To:

Your primary reader's email address

Cc: (Courtesy copy)

Enter your secondary reader's address. The primary and secondary readers will be able to each other's email addresses.

Bcc: (Blind courtesy copy)

The person whose address is placed here will be able to read your email but the people in 'To:' and 'Cc:' will not know that this person has been sent a copy.
This is often used for reasons of confidentiality.

Subject:

Short 'Headline' to grab your reader's attention and ensure your reader knows you sent them an email.

Body: Five basic parts:

1. **Salutation**
2. **Opening paragraph**
3. **Detail paragraphs** [Only when needed]
4. **Closing paragraph**
5. **Complimentary close**

Attachments:

Tells your reader what attachments have been sent using the file name. Also lets your reader know which programme was used to create each attachment.

Some tips on attachments and long emails

Sometimes you may have to include lots of details and data in your email.

Instead of putting all this detail directly into your email you might like to try:

✓ Using an attachment to contain the detail, so your email can be kept short and your reader can get the main point without reading through all the detail first.

✓ Placing the detail after the signature block. Your email can then be kept short and your reader can get the main point without reading through all the detail first.

✓ Always indicate to your reader in the closing where any detail might be located.

Deciding on the salutation:

The salutation usually begins with a greeting followed by a personal title such as Mr., Ms., or Dr. Use Ms. for a woman no matter what her marital status.

If there is a possibility that the person to whom you are writing is a Dr. or has some other title, use that title. Usually, people will not mind being addressed by a higher title than they actually possess, but try to be accurate.

Use the person's Family name if you use a title, e.g. Mr. Smith, Dr. Brown. If you know the person well and typically address them by their first name, it is acceptable to use the first name only in the salutation (e.g., Dear Lucy,) but no title should be used.

In all other cases, however, use the personal title and family name followed by a comma *(BE) or colon. *(AE)

If you don't know your reader's gender, use the full name. For example, you might write Dear Pat Brown, if you were unsure of Pat's gender.

Examples of basic salutations and their corresponding complimentary closes

	Formal	Informal
Salutation	Dear Mr. Jones:	Dear Brian,
	Dear Ms. Bryant:	Dear Joan,
	Dear Pat Smythe:	Dear Pat,
Complimentary Close	**Use with**	**Use with**
	Sincerely,	Kind regards,
	Regards,	Best regards,
	Best regards,	Regards,

*In British English (BE) the comma is used in the salutation, but in American English (AE) the colon is normal.

Body

Opening paragraph:

In the first paragraph, be friendly and positive, and then state the main purpose of your email. Remember that conciseness is very important.

Detail paragraph(s):

(Only needed if the opening and closing paragraphs do not give your reader enough information to take action.)

These paragraphs should justify the importance of the main point, give supporting details, and lead your reader into the last paragraph.

Closing paragraph:

The last paragraph should state what your reader should do, plus a positive statement about the future. Leave one blank line between each paragraph.

Complimentary close

This is a closing phrase, which indicates to your reader that your email is complete. It is similar to a greeting but at the end of your email.

Capitalise the first word only (e.g., Best regards) and put the sender's name and company position under it. A comma should follow the complimentary close.

	Formal	Informal
Complimentary Close	Sincerely,	Regards,
	Regards,	Kind regards,
	Kind regards,	Best regards,
Salutation	**Use with**	**Use with**
	Dear Mr. Jones:	Dear Brian,
	Dear Ms. Bryant,	Dear Joan,
	Dear Chris Smith:	Dear Chris,

© 2011 Alain Greaves ~ easystepsbusinessenglish.com ~ EFL EasySteps Series

EXERCISE ANSWER SUGGESTIONS:

There are often several ways to reword the examples, so the sentences given are only suggestions.

Exercises from page 41

We wish to announce our new product range.

You might like to look at our new product range.

We will be happy to email the contract details.

You will receive the contract details by email so you can get the project moving quickly.

We must have your proposal immediately.

Please let us have your proposal immediately so we can make a decision.

Exercises from page 43

I want you to come to our office next week.

Please visit our office next week.

I recommend you to call Mr. Jones at ABC.

Try calling Mr. Jones at ABC, as he might be interested/able to help.

We expect you to deliver on time.

Please deliver on time so we can meet our customer's deadline.

We can meet you in Munich at the exhibition.

Let's meet at the exhibition in Munich.

Exercises from page 46

You misunderstood the specifications.

Please check the following specifications.

You failed to include the sample.

Please send a sample so that we can make a decision.

You must meet our deadline.

Please make sure you meet the deadline, because…

You can't attend the meeting on Friday.

The meeting on Friday is only for the sales staff. Let's meet on Thursday so that…

You didn't complete the order.

There are some items missing from the order and we would appreciate your help to meet the deadline.

You told us the attachment was corrupted.

I have checked and resent the attachment that you told us was corrupted.

You should send us the data we want.

Please send the data we requested so that…

You should work with us on the ABC problem.

Let's work together on the ABC problem so that…

© 2011 Alain Greaves ~ easystepsbusinessenglish.com ~ EFL EasySteps Series

Your information is wrong.

Could you please send us the latest details as the information you sent is not what we expected?

You confused me with your report.

Could you please clarify the parts marked in yellow on the report you sent me, so that...?

You made a mistake on the contract.

The part marked on the contract doesn't seem to match what we agreed. Would you please check it and let me have an amended copy?

You are requested to complete the attached form.

Please complete the attached form so that...

You forgot to send the attachment.

Please send me a copy of the attachment you mentioned in your email.

Exercises from page 51

You are requested to activate the contract by signing the enclosed copy and returning it to us promptly.

Please sign and return the contract so that we can start the project quickly.

The specifications are inadequate and we expect you to give us more detail.

As soon as you give us more detailed specifications we can make a decision.

You made a mistake in your calculations and you have to work with us to put them right.

Our calculations are different from yours so let's work together to make them agree.

We can't make a decision unless you give us all the information we need.

We will make a decision as soon as you let us have the necessary information.

We won't be able to deliver on time unless you send us the Letter of Credit quickly.

Please send us the Letter of Credit quickly so that we can deliver on time.

Exercises from page 54

We cannot deliver the order until July 21.

Your order can be delivered on July 21.

Your specifications are incomplete so we are unable to make a decision.

We will be able to make a decision as soon as you send the complete specifications.

We are sorry to say, but we cannot reduce the price more than 7%.

You will receive up to 7% reduction in your quoted price.

You didn't give us all the details so we can't quote on the project.

We will quote on the project as soon as you give us all the details.

Because your terms were not in writing, we cannot accept responsibility for the breakages.

If your terms had been in writing we would have been able to accept responsibility for the breakages.

We cannot allow you to return this equipment because it has been damaged.

If the equipment had not been damaged we would have been able to allow you to return it.

Your quotation was delayed so we cannot submit it for consideration.

If your quotation had been on time we would have been able to submit it for consideration.

Unless you agree to our terms you will not be able to import these goods.

We will be able to import these goods provided you can agree to our terms.

You can learn how to make better use of the English you already know and how to become one of the BEST communicators in English.

For more information about the
EasySteps Series of ESL / EFL books, DVDs
and Business English materials
contact
alain@easystepsbusinessenglish.com

or go to

www.easystepsbusinessenglish.com

www.ingramcontent.com/pod-product-compliance
Lightning Source LLC
Chambersburg PA
CBHW071229050326
40689CB00011B/2499